LETTERS TO JODY

LETTERS TO JODY

Thomas D. Parks

TYNDALE HOUSE PUBLISHERS
Wheaton, Illinois

Coverdale House Publishers Ltd.
London, England

*Library of Congress Catalog Card Number 74-156897
SBN 8423-2166-7 Copyright © 1971 by Tyndale House
Publishers, Wheaton, Illinois 60187. All rights reserved.
Printed in the United States of America.*

First Printing, October 1971

To my daughter
Joanne Elizabeth

The following letters were written to a girl who had just entered a large state university. The teacher of her young people's Bible class in her church back home, an industrial scientist with a Ph.D. in chemistry, is the writer of the letters. When Jody left for State, she asked Dr. Blake if she could write to him and share her problems; to this he gladly agreed.

September 12

Dear Jody,

Thank you so much for your letter with all of the news of your arrival at State U. I think from now on I won't spend time thanking you for your letters and please don't thank me for mine so we will have more time to write about more important things.

Your room sounds good and I hope your roommate will turn out to be better than your first impression. Still waters run deep and perhaps as you get to know her she'll be a good friend. I don't think you should be surprised that you find State a little overwhelming. Even though there seem to be crowds of people everywhere you go, you'll probably find it's hard to make friends and get to know people. One of the mistakes students often make when they go away to school is to feel they must get to know lots and lots of people; they usually end up really knowing hardly anyone. It's better to have many acquaintances but few intimate friends. Someone has said, "A perfect friend is the one who knows the worst about you and loves you just the same." Whatever your circumstances, you will find few people like that.

I'm sure you remember you're now attending my wife's alma mater. I think we will try to make Homecoming this year, so we'll have a chance to visit with you and see your room and meet some of the girls in the dorm. Could you send me the football schedule, or at least tell me who State is playing at Homecoming?

Everything goes on as usual here but we are missing you and the others who have left for college, and our Bible class is going to have to develop some new leadership. Perhaps with the older kids gone some of the others will start to speak up and show more interest. I hope so. Write again soon and I will do my best to answer you.

Cordially,
Dr. Blake

September 20

Dear Jody,

I am delighted to have your enthusiastic letter after your first week of classes. You're certainly right that there is a terrific amount of information to learn and that at least part of the reason of your being at school is to come in contact with the great store of knowledge in the world. One of the things that impresses me is how this knowledge is exploding and how much more there is to learn now than when I was in the university. I don't remember whether I told you about the trip I took last fall back to my university to attend a dinner in honor of one of my old professors. In his little speech of acknowledgment of the occasion he made the observation that he came to the university to teach thirty years ago and that ninety percent of what he is now teaching wasn't even known then. His estimate pretty well confirms the usual statement that our store of knowledge is doubling every ten years, which means you have eight times as much factual knowledge to master now as I had thirty years ago.

Before I scare you like this, I should probably ask you if you have decided on a major. What I have said about the knowledge explosion is really more applicable, of course, to the fields of physical science than to the liberal arts. In fact, some areas of electronics and physics probably have a greater growth rate than this, but fields like history, literature, and languages are much slower. We had a visit last week from a friend who is a professor of medieval history at a state university out West. He is on his way to Europe where he will be spending a sabbatical in libraries in London, Paris, Rome, and Athens, reading old manuscripts to gather data on a particular man who lived in the twelfth century. I remember when he was with me at the university many years ago; just to do his thesis research for the Ph.D. he had to master Latin, Greek, Hebrew, and German. We can't expect a knowledge explosion in his area.

Don't let the atmosphere at the university lull you into the easy assumption that soon we will know everything and be able to solve all our problems. Seriously, there are limits to our knowledge. This is true whether we take the world of small things and run into the principle of uncertainty as we get down into the realm of electrons, or if we go to the other extreme and try to find the outer reaches of the universe, where we are thwarted again in our effort to gain absolute knowledge. I don't mean to get off on elementary epistimology, but I do hope that you keep the proper perspective in your study. Remember the verse in the Psalms: "His understanding (knowledge) is infinite." Perhaps Tennyson had this in mind when he wrote:

"Let knowledge grow from more to more,
But more of reverence in us dwell,
That mind and soul according well
May make one music as before,
But vaster."

Sincerely,
Dr. Blake

September 23

Dear Jody,

Thanks for the football schedule. The Homecoming game looks fine and we will plan to go. I don't know how many of Mrs. Blake's friends will be back, but we will enjoy it anyway; I hope the weather is good.

I was interested but not surprised to hear that you have succumbed to the "freshman syndrome." Being a little frog in a big pond hits nearly everyone who goes to a big school for the first time. I think that's true whether it is grade school, high school, or university. It's not surprising that most of the girls in the dorm are feeling the same way and some of them are asking deep questions about the meaning of life. Who am I? Why am I here? Is there any significance in being? I used to have a roommate who would look up from his book every once in a while and ask me, "How do you know this isn't a mental institution? How do you know we weren't sent here?" He was being facetious, but I think many kids feel as trapped and as frustrated as if they were behind bars in an asylum.

It would be easy to explain the frustration if it were confined to college kids, but I find it among my associates too. There is a general feeling of "What's the use? . . . Why the rat race?" I hear it expressed almost daily. I guess the word which most accurately describes the general attitude is despair. It's interesting that this malaise comes to us in a period of unprecedented affluence, when we possess more of every material thing than any other civilization has ever had. How much do you think this is contributing to the feelings of the kids in your dorm?

Perhaps the frustrations expressed by your friends are only a cover-up for a spiritual hunger which they don't want to admit. I think you will find that every generation has had the desire to do something great to contribute to the welfare of mankind and to leave the world better than they found it. Now it seems all of the frontiers have been conquered, there is no more land to settle or islands to subjugate — even walking on the moon is old hat — and after all this, young people are realizing that there is a spiritual vacuum which baffles them. I think you could be a help if you would quietly push them to face spiritual values in their lives.

Keep on keeping on,
Dr. Blake

September 28

Dear Jody,

Your letter about the dorm discussion was most interesting and especially the follow-up conversation you have had privately with some of the girls. Now you want to get behind the despair and try to understand the reason for it.

I think one of the prime causes of despair among young people today is what C. S. Lewis calls "the modern myth of evolutionism." He has an excellent treatment of this in *The World's Last Night*. I forget whether or not I have loaned this to you, but I know that we have discussed part of it in our Bible class. If you haven't read it maybe you should; I think you would enjoy it and I know it would be helpful. Very briefly, he describes the myth of progress which states that everything is moving toward perfection and that every day in every way the world is getting better. This has been fed to your university friends since they were little kids reading cartoons on cereal boxes. So it is no wonder that they accept it as a basic truth and as American as apple pie. However, now that they have been uprooted from the comfortable surroundings of their homes and neighborhoods, they find the world is very different. It's not getting better. There is crime and injustice and bigotry. There is war and danger of war in many parts of the world and a cry for revolutions at home. Small wonder that this generation is confused and looking for an escape.

Jody, we tried to hammer this home in our Bible class and I hope you never forget it. The root cause of our troubles at home and abroad is sin. I know that's an old-fashioned word, but the fact remains that in its biblical sense it means that we all fall short of God's standard of perfection. I think this is why it's so thrilling to be a Christian in these days — a Christian is a person who has faced the fact that he needs help and that Christ is the answer to his need. It is only when we are trusting in Christ that we can unselfishly live for others. I am sorry I can't write you a longer letter. I think perhaps you had some hidden questions and I'll try to get back to you soon.

Sincerely,
Dr. Blake

September 30

Dear Jody,

I wrote you a couple of days ago, but I have just reread your last letter and want to add something. I think the question that's really bothering you is, "How can God take any notice of me, only one person out of more than three billion people on a planet which is only one speck in the uncounted billions of stars in the universe?" You find yourself in an impersonal mass of 25,-000 students where you are identified by an IBM number on your ID card. You know very few students and few of them seem to recognize you as a person. So naturally it is easy to say in despair, "How could God possibly know or care about poor little me?" But that's exactly what you shouldn't say.

Remember the verse in the Psalms I gave you

in one of my previous letters: "His understanding is infinite." You must not limit God by the finite limits he has placed upon us. Don't think of him as a being like us only greater in every way. He is entirely different. He is the Creator and the Sustainer of the universe — of every galaxy, every star, every planet, every person, every molecule, and every electron. His understanding is infinite. I think that's what our Lord wanted us to understand when he assured us that even the hairs on our heads are numbered and known by our Father. So please don't think you are lost to his care because you seem to be submerged in the crowd at the university; he knows all about you, cares for you as a person, and loves you no less just because he also knows three billion others in the same way.

The old theologians were perfectly correct when they taught that Christ died for all mankind, but that he would have died for one person if it could have been possible for that one to be the only soul in the world.

Best wishes,
Dr. Blake

Dear Jody,

I am surprised at your reaction to my chance remark about the myth of evolutionism. I thought you knew me better than that. I wasn't attacking evolution as a theory; I merely pointed out that part of the frustration of young people today is caused by the painful realization that the world is not getting "better every day in every way."

I think one of our problems is the word "evolution" itself. It is used in many different ways and it seldom produces the same reaction in any two people who hear it. I am often asked by young people who know I am a scientist, "Do you believe in evolution?" I try to avoid a direct answer, not because I want to equivocate, but because unless I know what a person means by "evolution" or "believe in evolution," any answer can lead to more confusion. Did you notice the question: "Do you *believe* in evolution?" A scientist never uses the word "believe" about something he *knows* to be true. A chemist would never say, "I believe chlorine is poisonous," or "I believe oxygen supports combustion." The use of the word "believe" by a scientist doesn't indicate that he knows something but that a statement represents the best theory at the present time.

Remember when my friend Dr. Blast was in town and spoke to our class about his research on the age of the earth and the meteorites? Before men landed on the moon and brought back rock samples, he told me, "I believe the moon is as old as the earth." I visited him after he had tested the actual samples and he told me exactly what his measurements on the age of the rocks had indicated. He didn't state this as something to be believed, but as something he knew as a scientific fact. So I wonder, when people ask me, "Do you believe in evolution?", if they realize that they are asking for a statement of faith. This takes the whole question out of the scientific realm into the religious in the sense of a leap into the dark.

You haven't mentioned a Bible class or a church. Have you found some place where you can be active and happy? Please let me know what you are doing.

Sincerely,
Dr. Blake

Dear Jody,

You are persistent! I thought I had disposed of your concern about evolution but I guess I'll have to try harder. As you know, my training is not in biology and I try to be careful not to overstep the bounds of my experience. In fact, as you know from our discussions in class, I feel that many well-meaning people have done much harm by attacking evolution when they haven't had facts to support their arguments. Often they speak out of an abundance of ignorance and I don't want to fall into that pit.

The theory of evolution appears to be a good working hypothesis and to be very useful in teaching the biological sciences. I think the problem comes when people forget it is a theory and accept it as dogma. I recently read the symposium papers on the "Origin of Life" which were edited by Professor Oparin of Russia. You may remember he startled the scientific world about fifteen years ago with a new theory of origins.

In reading this work I was impressed with two things; first, the vagueness of the presentation, and this became more noticeable as the authors were forced to face details; and second, the apparent willingness of the participants to accept as fact statements which were earlier presented as unproven theories. I think that many of the scientists I know who embrace a total evolutionary system do so because they choose to believe that way. In other words it has become for them a religion with its elements of faith to cover the gaps rather than a reasoned scientific position as they would like to have you believe.

I know I have to be careful when I talk like this or I can be accused of being an obscurantist or of having religious prejudice. I guess it's difficult for anyone to take a position which is completely free of prejudice either in basic assumptions or in the conclusion he draws. Please believe me, Jody — my religious faith involves a sincere desire for truth and I have every confidence that if we maintain such an attitude the theories which are tried and discarded will eventually aid in our quest. I think it's important to keep an open mind but it's just as important that we critically evaluate what we hear and what we read so we're not led down too many blind alleys. Keep thinking, though, and keep in touch.

> Sincerely,
> Dr. Blake

Dear Jody,

I certainly don't recommend that you spend a lot of time trying to read both sides of the question of evolution. There are dozens of books written attacking Darwin's theory but these are of varying quality and it seems to me that most of them are written to help confirm those who reject any value in the theory and have little effect on those who want to accept it. When you come home at Christmas you can browse through my library and pick out what you want to read.

There is something I think you should read, however, and it appears in a very interesting place. It's the Introduction to Darwin's *Origin of Species* in the 100th Anniversary Edition of Everymans Library published by J. M. Dent in London and E. P. Dutton in New York. I'm sure your library at school will have a copy. The author is the director of the Commonwealth Institute of Biological Control in Canada. Objections to many of the key assumptions of Darwin's theory have been raised many times, but not, in my reading, with such telling effect or by one so well informed as the author of this Introduction. Let me know your reaction after you've read it.

For my part, I'm still willing to accept the story of Genesis by faith without trying to accommodate it into any particular theory, or what is probably more common, to accommodate a scientific theory to Genesis. There is still so much we don't know. Perhaps this is one of the areas where we just have to be patient and wait for a better understanding. In the meantime, be careful not to get enamored with the myth of evolutionism!

I would love to hear more about your courses and your professors.

Sincerely,
Dr. Blake

Dear Jody,

I am glad to get your letter about the courses you're taking and about some of your professors. I think you are wise to settle on a major right away and then to build your plans for graduation around it. So many kids seem to flounder and end up in their senior year without requirements in one area or another.

Dr. Clark, your English professor, really seems to have you upset. You mentioned so many things about him that I can't put my finger on your real complaint. I hope you aren't prejudiced because he has long hair and a beard — really superficial things. Are you upset with him because he is an outspoken unbeliever or do you feel he is hitting below the belt when he uses class time to attack the Christian faith?

Often when a person goes out of his way to make remarks about spiritual things, even when these remarks are cynical or antagonistic, it shows a hidden interest and a confession of need. Don't expect your Dr. Clark to admit this, though, even to himself. Wouldn't it be interesting to know why he is so bitter? Who helped warp his life? His parents, a friend, a Sunday school teacher? I like Thomas Merton's calm advice, "Do not be too quick to condemn the man who no longer believes in God: for it may be your own coldness and avarice and mediocrity and materialism and sensuality and selfishness that have killed his faith."

Why don't you try to have a positive approach in the class discussion? Instead of getting angry with him and blowing your top, you could use the opportunity to present your faith in class. After all, if he raises the subject, he's certainly asking for a rebuttal and perhaps down deep this is what he wants. I know the professor has the upper hand, but if you pray for opportunities and trust the Lord for wisdom, you will find this a very interesting experience.

Be on the ready,
Dr. Blake

Dear Jody,

I gather Dr. Clark can put down just about anyone with his caustic wit, but again I would suggest that you be patient and try to realize that this may be a front for a troubled heart. One point at which I would have difficulty with Dr. Clark is his statement that university courses are taught with an objective approach to knowledge in contrast with the subjectivity of religion. I had very little contact with English professors, so I can't really speak with any authority about them, but I know that not all of my science courses were taught with pure objectivity. Much of what we learned (and got good grades for putting on an exam paper) is now completely out of date. I had one dear old professor of chemistry who was determined to find a missing element in the periodic table; he drew conclusions and published results in all sincerity. His problem was that he was so emotionally involved that he couldn't look at the facts objectively. He died a broken, disappointed man when his work was disproved by others. Then I was taught in physics that it was absolutely impossible to fly an airplane faster than the speed of sound. We got full credit for repeating this "objective" truth.

Dr. Clark would be a rare bird indeed if he approached his subject without some subjective feeling. Suggest to him sometime that Shakespeare didn't write *Julius Caesar* or *Macbeth,* and see how he reacts! But remember that behind the beard and the debonair agnosticism there is a person who desperately needs the peace and comfort that only faith in Christ can give.

Sincerely,
Dr. Blake

October 30

Dear Jody,

I am glad to hear you spoke up in Dr. Clark's class. Why were you surprised that several others agreed with you? Please don't let him sell the intellectual demands of Christianity short.

I'm willing to leave Dr. Clark in his delusion that he teaches pure objective knowledge, but I don't think his attack on the reasonableness of the Christian faith should go unchallenged. Some of the greatest minds of history have struggled with its depth of meaning, and great men still bow in reverence before revealed truth. I recently read a book by Dr. William Pollard who is director of the Oak Ridge Institute of Nuclear Studies. He found Christ after he had completed his Ph.D. work in physics and was already a professor at a state university. He maintained his professional activity and research but took the theological courses required to qualify as a priest in the Episcopal Church. He states, without qualification, that the studies required for the priesthood were more rigorous and more demanding than those for the Ph.D. in physics.

Now Jody, I hope you won't think I'm saying that the Christian faith is totally an intellectual exercise. That would be silly; volition, emotion, trust, and commitment are all involved as well. But since Dr. Clark attacks it as unreasonable or anti-intellectual, it is good to realize that it is he who is being not quite objective in his judgment. The people and events the Bible describes were real, and where secular history and archaeology intersect with the biblical record there is remarkable correspondence. In addition, there is what Dr. Francis Schaeffer calls the "mannishness of man" which is displayed throughout the Bible. We can understand the actions and the attitudes of Bible characters, even from earliest times, because they are like us. This gives special meaning to the incarnation: Jesus Christ was born of Mary in Bethlehem of Judea. He came into time and space and his contemporaries are known and documented — Herod the Tetrarch, Pilate, Caesar Augustus, Annas, John, Peter, Paul — but he was also contemporary with Abraham and Moses and he is contemporary with you and me today. I must close but I want to quote from Giovanni Papini who said, in recounting his life's experience, "It has happened often to Christ that He has been more tenaciously loved by the very men who hated Him at first. Hate is sometimes only imperfect and unconscious love: and in any case it is a better foundation for love than indifference."* So let us take heart and pray for Dr. Clark and all such.

Sincerely,
Dr. Blake

*From Papini's *Life of Christ* (New York: Harcourt, Brace and Co. and Grosset and Dunlap, 1925) p. 18.

Dear Jody,

I am so glad we had a chance to see you at Homecoming. As we talked on the way home, my wife remarked that it was too bad we didn't see more of you, but at least we can picture your daily routine now. We're already planning a reunion dinner at our house during Christmas vacation for all of the Bible class kids that are away at college. But in addition to this, I hope you will have time to come over and sit down and talk for a while.

I'm sorry I didn't have time to answer the question you asked as we walked to the car: "How can you ever think that Christ would have died for me if I were the only person in the world?" I remember telling you this in a letter and while it's a hypothetical statement, the point I was making was the worth God places on a human soul. But there is more than this involved, and that is the real, deep I-thou relationship between each of us and Christ. The Apostle Paul referred in one of his letters to ". . . the Son of God who loved me and gave himself for me." Here is the ultimate contrast to the depersonalization of modern society. Although we must never forget that Christ died for the sins of the world, it is only as I recognize the fact that he died for me personally that I appropriate the forgiveness and cleansing which is mine as a believer.

Sincerely,
Dr. Blake

November 14

Dear Jody,

I can just imagine the buzzing among the girls on your floor when someone found a contraceptive diaphragm in the washroom after the dorm party. The incident surprised me — I thought "the pill" had completely taken over.

I saw a TV panel discussion on premarital sex about two weeks ago. With only one exception, the panel was in favor of it. The moderator contended that sex experience before marriage resulted in a more successful and happier marriage and she didn't even limit the number of partners one could have. Frankly, Jody, as a scientist I am appalled at this kind of talk. How did she measure happiness or unhappiness in marriage? Does she have an analytical balance to weigh despair, or a machine to record hours of worry and sleeplessness? Does she have an intensity scale for happiness to rate each marriage? The answer is, of course, that she doesn't have any objective measure of these things and her statement which sounded so sophisticated on

TV was open to serious question.

Some of the panel members dressed up the inanity by putting "limits" on premarital sex — the kind one often hears: only have relations if you are in love with the other person; never have relations if it will hurt another person. First of all, this question of love is hard to pin down and it can become meaningless. A boy wants to sleep with a girl so he professes love for her; the next month he goes through the same profession for another girl who has caught his fancy. Even "going steady" doesn't guarantee a love relationship. You'll find lots of girls at State who go steady with two or three different guys in the course of a year. Does a girl love each of them? And does each qualify as a sex partner? Then comes the platitude about having relations only if it doesn't hurt another person. How does one know? How does one measure "hurt"? It seems to me that our biggest computer wouldn't be able to take into account all the possibilities of hurting a person by one act of intimacy. A human being is a delicate and sensitive thing, and when one considers the whole of life ahead with possible marriage and family, the chances for "hurt" are staggering. So if a fellow really loves a girl he will show it by waiting until the security of marriage; he will want to avoid any possibility of hurting the one he loves.

Sincerely yours,
Dr. Blake

November 20

Dear Jody,

I realize that when you listen to the girls in the dormitory, it sounds as if premarital sex were the accepted norm, especially among university co-eds, but please don't take this as fact. There is a recent report in the *Journal of the American Medical Association* on "Sex and Mental Illness on Campus" by a staff psychiatrist at a large state university health clinic. He is careful not to make judgmental conclusions, but he did present a number of interesting facts. He feels that although there is a revolution in expressed attitudes towards sex, there is little evidence that the incidence of premarital intercourse is radically changed. He quotes a number of clinical studies at other universities which agree with his findings that about 80 percent of undergraduate girls have not had this experience and that the percentage has remained the same since early studies in 1910. The author concluded that there is a wide gap between what girls may boast about and what they actually practice.

One of the interesting sidelights of the report was the disproportionate number of girls coming for psychiatric help who already had had one or more sex partners. While it used to be common for psychiatrists to belittle Christian sexual attitudes and to consider them an important cause of mental illness, the experience in this particular clinic indicated exactly the opposite. The author makes an observation which I wish could be read by any co-ed who feels tempted to take part in premarital sex: "I have never heard a single phrase from any student, male or female, which suggests that girls were more esteemed as important and worthwhile persons because of their enlightened sexual attitudes. At the same time, I have seen many patients who abandoned career aspirations once they began to be involved with multiple partners. Unfortunately, the sexually permissive girl comes to see herself as more of an object and less of an equal partner. At the same time, she is given more responsibility than ever before for prevention of pregnancy and is probably less able than girls of previous generations to count on the help of her boyfriend if she is impregnated. In effect, she is valued by men for her sexual capacities and for these alone."*

Keep listening, Jody, but don't be overimpressed by what you hear. And by all means, watch for opportunities to be of help to individuals who are floundering.

Sincerely yours,
Dr. Blake

*Seymour L. Halleck, M.D., "Sex and Mental Health on the Campus," *The Journal of the American Medical Association*, Vol. 200, No. 8, May 22, 1967, p. 687.

Dear Jody,

I had just mailed my last letter to you when I received a new book published by Inter-Varsity Press and edited by Gladys Hunt. I'm sending it to you. It's called *Listen to Me* and it presents the personal thoughts, aspirations, and philosophies of eight widely different college and university kids.

The story that bears directly on what the psychiatrist found in his clinic was written by Leslie, a southern belle who had used sex first as a means of getting attention and affection, then as a control over men, and finally as an expression of contempt. After two college years filled with a variety of sex partners, she transferred to a large university for her junior year. Here she came in contact with a Christian fellowship group and heard for the first time of forgiveness and the love of God; more important to her at the time, she was treated by the members of the group as a person, not as a thing to be used. She became a Christian during her junior year and found the fulfillment she had so desperately sought all her life.

She recounts her past, not to boast, but I'm sure in the sincere hope that others who read it will not go through the same sad experience. Did she love the various sex partners? She thought at the time she had loved the early ones, but now she knows she didn't. Did she get hurt in the experience? Yes — very deeply. She still doesn't know if she can ever marry and have a successful life. By all means, read the whole book, but read the chapter by Leslie first.

Remember when we discussed situation ethics in our Bible class? And how the Christian's behavior is determined, not by a particular situation, but by the authority of the Word of God? The instructions about sexual purity given to the early Church were valid for the immoral societies of Greece and Rome, and they are valid for life in this last third of the twentieth century. The plea is to avoid all forms of evil and to "run away from immorality," all of which is consistent with the high view that each human is a being of worth; one made in the image of God must not be treated as an object or a thing.

I could go on and talk of the beauty of Christian marriage, but I think I'll save that subject for a later time. In the meantime, remember that very likely there are many Leslies in your university, perhaps even in your dorm; be sure you have an open heart and that your fellowship group is a place where all are welcome.

Cordially yours,
Dr. Blake

Dear Jody,

I was delighted to hear about the Bible study which started in your dorm and especially pleased that the girls came and asked you to lead it. It's always better this way, rather than your forcing a study on them. I am worried about one thing, however, and that is your hope that the class will be a good source of kids for the campus Christian fellowship group. I think this study is worthwhile to have for itself. If anything else grows out of it, that is all the better, but don't for a moment let the girls feel that they are having attention paid to them for an ulterior motive. People hate this sort of thing and so would you if you were in their position. So many well-meaning Christians make this mistake; they say, "I must be friendly to Jane so I can win her to the Lord," and then they turn on the charm.

Trouble comes when Jane sees through the phoniness of the friendship and says, in effect, "I don't want anything to do with you or your Christ." What we should say is, "I want to be a friend of Jane's because she is a person I would really like to know," and then trust the Lord for the opportunity to share our faith as we get to know her.

Tell me a little more about the class. Are you going to study a book of the Bible or a topical subject? Are you going to use one of the printed lesson outlines? There are some excellent helps available, as you probably know. Don't worry about some of the girls who seem to give trouble in discussions; the Holy Spirit can use the Word in spite of and sometimes because of the digressions. I think we often like to control the way the Spirit does his work — perhaps in order that we can have the satisfaction of doing a good job — but our Lord warned us against this when he talked to Nicodemus: "The wind blows where it will; you hear the sound of it, but you do not know where it comes from or where it is going. So is everyone who is born of the Spirit." So, Jody, keep a firm hand on the discussion and always bring them back to the main point, but don't drive away any who disagree; and above all, pray that the Holy Spirit will use the Word to satisfy the need of each heart. Don't think for a moment you stand alone.

Pray much and stay humble,
Dr. Blake

Dear Jody,

Do I detect a suggestion that your Bible study in the dorm plus the fellowship meeting on campus should be all the church attendance you need for the week? I hope not, and I will tell you why. When the Apostle Paul wrote to the church at Corinth, he compared a local church to a human body — each member has a part to play (or a function to perform) just as do our hands, feet, taste buds, and eyes. Most simply, this example says to me that the local church is not meant to be monolithic, but that it should be of variety in makeup. Any student group tends to bring together people of the same age, social status, intellectual ability, and cultural interests, and to follow the example of the body used by Paul, the result is one organ rather than the whole functioning body.

A local church, in contrast, is composed of young and old, married and single, rich and poor, educated and uneducated. There are those who sing in the choir, those who usher, those who speak, and others who work behind the scenes, taking care of the finances. There are those who teach in Sunday school, others who work with young people, and some who take care of the nursery and cradle roll. Not only can a person like yourself learn much just by getting to know so many different kinds of people with their special gifts and special problems, but you have a great opportunity to help others because of your talents and the fact you are a university student. I know it sounds trite, but you need the local church, and it needs you.

Peace!
Dr. Blake

December 6

Dear Jody,

The question about how often you "should" attend church is difficult to answer. Frankly, I doubt that with the busy schedule you have you will attend more often than you should! In my college years I knew several guys who flunked out because they spent too much time in the bar or the theater or the gym, but I don't know anyone who failed as a result of going to church too often. If you decide to teach the Sunday school class that has been offered, you will get many benefits besides the satisfaction of helping a bunch of younger kids. You will learn a lot as you prepare your lesson and it will help you to get into a regular habit of being at church on time.

The excuses you are getting from the girls

for not wanting to go to church on Sunday are as old as the hills. One says, "I can worship sitting on a hillside watching the wonders of God's creation." Another, "It seems so forced to have to worship at the same time each Sunday morning; why can't I just worship when I really feel like it no matter where this is?" When we understand that worship is the appreciation of the "worthship" of God revealed in Christ, we shouldn't try to limit it to a particular time and place. However, because God knows our limitations, he has given some guidelines and helps for worship, and one of these is to come together as a body to encourage each other in singing, in prayer, and in the reading of the Word. The individual experience does not substitute for, neither does it preclude corporate worship.

Going to church isn't something you can force on anyone, nor is it something you should force if you could. However, you can encourage the girls in your dorm by your example. If you do, when student days are over I think you'll find you look back on your experience in the local church among the highlights of your university career. I found it so in my own university days.

Sincerely,
Dr. Blake

December 12

Dear Jody,

I was jolted by your last letter telling me the problems you are finding in the dorm with girls not wanting to go home for Christmas vacation. The most difficult thing to understand, of course, is the apparent deep-seated hatred some girls feel for their parents. Do they feel they can be popular in the dorm by attacking the establishment in this way or do they really object to the restraints that parents put on children? This is really a new phenomenon to me. I don't remember a single person in all of my college or university experience who ever expressed himself as hating his home or his parents. Could this be the new cause of much of the sickness of the "now generation"?

I don't expect to have another letter from you before your Christmas vacation starts, but I want to think a little about what you told me and I'll write you again soon.

Sincerely,
Dr. Blake

December 14

Dear Jody,

I'm still upset about your last letter, especially about the kids you have talked to who seem to hate their parents. As I told you, I didn't go through this and I didn't have any friends who did. I've been thinking a lot about it, however, and I think there are some things I can see from my perspective as a father and as a friend to many young people.

Do you realize that all new mothers and fathers start their tremendous responsibility largely without training, certainly without experience, and very often plagued by financial burdens? The emotional climate in the average home of a young couple with a new baby undoubtedly leads to much of the family problems that are found later. Another contributing factor to what you are seeing may be related to our materialistic culture which, especially after the Great Depression, has dominated American life. Very often both parents work to earn enough money to provide the material things they feel their children should have. As a consequence, neither has enough time to devote to the home or the children. Instead of a haven of love, the home becomes a place of irritation and conflict. I am sure many of your friends have been raised in families like this and although they have been provided with everything they've asked for in the way of clothes, travel, cars, and now college money, they perhaps feel that this is all done without love.

I am glad you are coming home and that your home is one where spiritual values have first place. I am looking forward to a good talk about this and many other things we have written about.

See you soon,
Dr. Blake

Dear Jody,

A week has already gone by since you left and although I promised to write you immediately, things have been hectic after the Christmas rush and I hope you'll understand. I'm sorry Mrs. Blake and I didn't have a chance to talk to you alone at greater length, but then, we didn't expect you to have Sandy with you for your whole vacation. I wonder if she will be helped by seeing the healthy relationship you have with your parents or if she'll feel more frustrated. I feel very sad about her and the many others in your dorm who feel the same way about their parents.

Do you feel that Sandy is really so upset about the materialism she sees in her home, or as she says, "the hypocritical standards of the establishment?" Do you think she feels there's any virtue at all in the way her parents have worked hard to provide her with everything and to send her to college? I wonder what she'll do when she has responsibility for her own children.

Please write me and tell me Sandy's reaction to her visit with you. She was quiet when she came to our Bible class, but I am sure she was thinking. I'll be interested in hearing if anything develops.

Have a good New Year,
Dr. Blake

Dear Jody,

So Sandy feels that Christians are even worse hypocrites than her parents and that they have a cloak of religion only to act as a cover for a safe life!

Unfortunately, much of what she says appears to be true and we just cannot dismiss it lightly. The English poet Wordsworth said, "The world is too much with us: late and soon, getting and spending we lay waste our powers." If it was true nearly two hundred years ago in England, it certainly is more true today in these United States. It seems that our lives are dominated by things, which after all is materialism. Even those of us who know in our hearts that "here we have no continuing city, but we seek one to come," are enmeshed in the spirit of this age. I think it's important that we admit this first to God, then to ourselves, and then to our critics, because a materialistic people is exactly the opposite of what our Lord intended us to be. Only as we face ourselves as we actually are will we start to do something about it.

I think a good place to start in your Bible study for this spring quarter would be the teaching of our Lord in the Sermon on the Mount. It is found in each of the first three Gospels, but the most complete version is the one in Matthew 5, 6, and 7. What our Lord taught was the highest ideal and what he demands is very difficult, but after all, Sandy and her friends seem to be asking for difficult things. Perhaps if she would get her eyes and thoughts off her fellow human beings and back to the Source, it would give her a new perspective. I will be glad to help with materials or advice if you ask. Let me know.

Sincerely yours,
Dr. Blake

Dear Jody,

Sandy didn't strike me as a person with deep concerns for social justice when she was here, but you say her main hang-up is with civil rights and the problems of the ghetto. Why does she feel all Christians are satisfied with the status quo and that Christian churches have flubbed in their duty to the city people? She may be right, but I wonder if she's spent any time in the ghetto, taking part in any agencies that are helping — or is she merely cranking through a cracked record? And even more important perhaps, could this attack possibly be another cover-up for her own personal inadequacy and failure? Maybe you'll learn the answers as you have more talks with her.

If Sandy were alone in her feelings about

Christians and social issues, we could pass off her criticisms a lot more easily, I guess. The truth is, there is a growing swell of young intelligent people who believe just as Sandy does. I think it should challenge us to go back to our beginnings and rethink our Christian position. By definition, every true Christian is a person who has made a declaration against the status quo. He had to be dissatisfied with himself, with his prospects in the world, and with his hope of the future, before he came to Christ. A big problem is that so many people have just drifted into a Christian position and never have had a real crisis experience of repentance and a changed life. I am not sure this argument would satisfy Sandy because I am sure she could point to many people who claim new life and yet show no concern for social justice.

Try to give me some help in my thinking. Maybe one way to do this would be to give me some feedback on what she says when you present her need to trust Christ. I hope you can do it soon and I will await your letter with anticipation.

Wait on the Lord and trust him,
Dr. Blake

Dear Jody,

I am glad you remembered the discussion we had in our Bible class about the social reformers in the Evangelical Movement of England. I think the Christian leadership in abolition of slavery, prison reform, in building hospitals, and establishing many other agencies to alleviate suffering is a very powerful argument for the proof of general Christian concern for social justice. But Sandy is quite unimpressed with things that happened a hundred years ago: "What have you done for us today?" We'll have to admit we aren't doing much, but maybe we should start. Why not have your Bible study group take an afternoon a week to teach remedial reading to the children in the ghetto? This would be a positive witness and an outlet to practice some of the things you're learning.

Maybe later you could do something with the teen-agers. Perhaps you could find some way to have a place — some kind of youth center — where they could come and feel welcome. Just a chance to talk about serious things is very important to them. This would be a lot of work and involvement and perhaps you would need some outside help, but it's a thought. I'm sure you will think of some other things but if you want an answer for Sandy, I think some action would be better than words. What are your ideas?

Sharing your concern,
Dr. Blake

Dear Jody,

I can't tell you how glad I am that you've gotten to know some of the black students on campus. One thing that concerns me is that the only ones you mention are guys. Do you know any black girls? I think it would be a good idea if you would make a special effort to get to know some of the girls because they have a point of view that may be a lot easier for you to understand as a girl. Besides, your friend-liness may be misunderstood if it's so one-sided. I'm not surprised at the depth of feeling you have heard expressed about the racial situation, but I think it shows how big a factor it is in their lives — you're fortunate to be close enough to them that they feel free to vent their feelings.

I'm surprised that you wonder at the generalizations and blanket condemnation they make about white people. After all, whites do the same thing about blacks. I'm sure I'm guilty even though I try to keep the fact in front of me that each person is a separate individual and must not be forced into a racial mold.

Unfortunately, many of the things are true that your black friends tell you about the racial injustice their people have suffered. I'm glad you're concerned about what you can do about it and how you can show them that you're trying to understand and that you really care. You can't change the attitude of all white Americans, but you can be sure that you are right in your own heart; you can treat each person you come in contact with — regardless of his color — as a person with dignity, made in the image of God. Have we ever discussed the fact that only biblical Christianity gives a sound rationale for the dignity of man? Remember, Jesus Christ was not an Anglo-Saxon, blue-eyed, blond, Protestant Savior — he was the man for all times and all people.

Let me know how things are coming along.

Dr. Blake

Dear Jody,

I know I haven't really given you time to reply to my last letter, but there are a couple of things I would like to add. A lot of criticism has been directed toward our racial attitude in the United States, and maybe because we are so close to the situation, we tend to think that racism is our exclusive problem. It isn't. As a matter of fact, it is probably one of the major driving forces down through the centuries that has helped to make the ethnic groupings which we have in the world today. There was racism in early Egypt when the local people had contempt for the shepherds of the desert. Many feel that one of Jonah's big problems was racial when he didn't want to go to Nineveh. And our Lord certainly faced the problem in Samaria when he sat down and talked to a woman from the despised people with whom the Jews had no dealings whatsoever.

When Mrs. Blake and I were in Hawaii last spring I was quite surprised to find deep racial animosities in the much touted melting-pot of the Pacific. A native pastor told me about the problems of a Chinese girl who was engaged to a Japanese in his church. Both families — both faithful members of the church — had come to him separately to plead that he dissuade the two from going through with the marriage. This seems strange to us, because many Occidentals can't easily tell the difference between the two races. I'm sure there are other examples, but I don't want you to think I'm trying to justify the racism which exists in our country. I do see encouraging signs of a changing attitude among young people and this may be one of the real contributions your generation makes to understanding among people. The fact that you were able to talk with your black student friends frankly about these problems is indicative of a change in outlook. There's a lot more I could say, but I'll wait till I hear from you again. It'll probably be good for you to collect your thoughts and write them down.

Yours,
Dr. Blake

Dear Jody,

I hope our understanding of the racial problem doesn't have to wait till your professor set-
tles the question of heredity and environment.
Of course, I agree with you that cultural differences are important, but how they are related
to genetic differences and races, I don't think
we know yet. You probably know about the
current trauma in educational circles because
some psychologists claim they have proof that
genetic differences lead to certain races having a
lower I.Q. than others. It looks like this subject
is going to be debated for many years and I
won't be surprised if our whole basis for I.Q.
testing is challenged and changed as a result.
What appears to be intelligence in one area may
be useless in a different situation. I remember
my anthropology professor's telling us that if an
aboriginal of Australia were transported immediately and placed in Times Square, he would

probably go crazy. After the professor had allowed enough time for the class to sit back and smugly agree on our superiority, he then said, "And if any of you were transported immediately and dropped in the outback of Australia, you would do the same."

The cultural gap is real. I used to live in a town bordering on Appalachia. I tried to help in a church which ministered to people who had come up to work in our city, but I found it almost impossible to communicate with them. We were the same color, we had the same racial background, we even had the same basic Christian outlook, but the difference in our cultures seemed too great to overcome. I know the same thing is true of young people from the ghettos who "educate themselves out of their environment" and find it almost impossible to go back and relate to their own people.

Everything I have said above is in agreement with your statements about cultural differences, and I'm not sure it's very helpful. I think you and your Christian group at the university have a wonderful opportunity to prove the reality of the biblical position that "in Christ there are no differences between Greek and Jew . . . barbarian and Scythian, slave and freeborn." This is an essential message of the gospel — don't let side issues detract you from this powerful truth.

God is faithful,
Dr. Blake

Dear Jody,

I hope we can get on to another subject in our letters but I must answer your direct question about my claim that biblical Christianity gives the only true basis for the dignity of man. I want to mention two things the Bible teaches about all men. First, we are created in the image and likeness of God. Now, don't think of an old man in the sky who looks like your grandfather's uncle — that's not the point at all. It isn't physical image, but our spiritual being that's meant — our will, our intelligence, and our emotions, the things that go to make up personality. We as men are able to think God's thoughts after him and to communicate with him because he made us like himself. The second thing the Bible teaches about all men is that we are descendants of one set of parents, Adam and Eve, and this point also bears on the dignity of all men because if we are all related, all brothers, there is no room for inferior or superior races. I think the Apostle Paul summed it all up very well when he talked to the Greek philosophers in Athens: "From one forefather, he has created every race of men to live over the face of the whole earth." Remember when we studied the incarnation in Bible class? Christ became man and is related to each of us and as man he is the visible likeness of the invisible God.

You see, Jody, the minute we depart from the biblical position and accept a total evolutionary development of man, we no longer have first parents in common nor do we have an explanation for the spiritual nature of man. The Bible is consistent in its unyielding declaration of the worth of each person and the responsibility that each has to his Creator — for there is no difference; "All have sinned and come short of the glory of God." When Christ came into the world, he came to save sinners — all mankind irrespective of race, color, education, or economic position. And when he died, he died for all mankind.

Dr. Blake

Dear Jody,

The only thing that surprises me about your letter on drugs is that it didn't come a long time ago. To answer your first question, I think you ought to be able to find more worthwhile things to do on campus than taking part in demonstrations either for or against new drug laws. One of the problems with such activities is that when you're demonstrating, you rarely know what's going on and sometimes the leaders have mixed motives. Often you'll put in a lot of time and effort and find that the results are something you had never anticipated. I wonder how many of the kids who have been drawn into a demonstration are really pleased with the violence, the burning, and the bombing that have resulted. Why not try instead to be an instrument of peace? Could you find something positive to do with your Christian friends to counteract the destructive elements?

Now to your second question. Yes, I'll admit my generation has a problem with alcohol, and I'll even admit there are some inconsistencies in the laws covering nonhabit-forming drugs (if there are such things as nonhabit-forming drugs — who knows?). But all of this taken together doesn't justify the use of drugs by young people. There's something very disappointing and sad about a student generation hiding behind parents' mistakes to indulge in a drug culture. Have you read the sermon given by Malcolm Muggeridge when he resigned as Rector of the University of Edinburgh? The whole thing is a masterful piece, but I want to quote just a few lines because I think they bear on your question: "The students here in this University, as in other universities, are the ultimate beneficiaries under our welfare system. They are supposed to be the spearhead of progress, flattered and paid for by their admiring seniors, an élite who will happily and audaciously carry the torch of progress into the glorious future opening before them . . . Yet how infinitely sad; how, in a macabre sort of way, funny that the form their insubordination takes should be a demand for pot and pills, for the most tenth rate sort of escapism and self-indulgence ever known! It is one of those situations a social historian with a sense of humour will find very much to his taste. All is prepared for a marvellous release of youthful creativity; we await the great works of art, the high-spirited venturing into new fields of perception and understanding — and what do we get? The resort of any old slobbering debauchee anywhere in the world at any time — dope and bed."*

Sincerely,
Dr. Blake

*Malcolm Muggeridge, *Jesus Rediscovered,* (Wheaton, Ill.: Tyndale House Publishers, 1971), pp. 54, 55.

March 20

Dear Jody,

What a letter! Not a word about Sandy, racism, the drug scene, or your Bible study — the only things you talked about were your inadequacies and failures. My first reaction was relief to find out that you're made of the same stuff as the rest of us. I think every Christian should stop and take stock of his motives and goals and especially of his relationship to the Lord.

Jody, please believe me when I tell you that the war you find going on inside is common to every sincere believer. You mentioned Romans 7, so I don't have to tell you to read Paul's experience — but I would like to remind you that the great apostle moved out of Chapter 7 into Chapter 8. I strongly recommend that you dwell for a while on the truths of Romans 8. God has justified us by faith, he has given us peace, he has promised that nothing can separate us from him — and all of this because of what Jesus Christ has done for us. Perhaps your problem is that you feel that you've been fighting the battle alone on so many fronts. Please believe me, Jody, you're not alone. Christ has begun a good work in you and he will complete it.

I don't want to seem unsympathetic, and above all I don't want to be trite, but if you are going to be a useful ambassador for Christ on the campus, it is essential that you confess your weakness and accept Christ's strength. Simply rest in the Lord and on his finished work. I hope you won't take that to be preacherish or theological, because I mean it to be very practical. In my own experience, I've found that looking at Christ instead of myself is the secret of a happy and balanced Christian life. I hope you'll give it a chance.

Let me know how you're coming along.

Dr. Blake

Dear Jody,

I am glad to hear that you had already moved into the eighth chapter of Romans before my letter reached you and that what I said sort of made sense. It's hard to look at the subject objectively because it seems like we're always either in Chapter 7 or Chapter 8, but it's good to have an idea of what's happening, so that if you fall back into Chapter 7, you know to strive for Chapter 8.

Getting back to your question about the use of drugs on campus, I think there are probably three contributing factors which lead to widespread use of drugs today. First, it's the "in" thing — the way to make yourself look good in the group. Maybe that's because it's against the law and so there's a certain thrill of doing something that's forbidden, but I think mostly that kids who don't want to be considered out of it and want very much to be accepted by their friends, will smoke pot for no other reason than that. A second reason I think is that a lot of kids look for an escape just the way that many of their parents turn to alcohol. They find the pressures of society too great, and they welcome an easy way out. Usually they start with pot, but after a while they may find that they need something more, so they graduate to hallucinogenics and finally to hard drugs. There is a third reason (which I am convinced has the deepest psychological roots of all) and that is that many take a trip on LSD or other hallucinogenic drugs in their desire for meaning. They want in some way to find reality or to find God. What they do find often are bizarre and horrible nightmares which have led to some of the most gruesome suicides and crimes in our generation. But this doesn't change the original purpose and desire of those taking the trip.

These are my observations from the drug users I have talked with. I'm really interested to hear what you have found there on campus. Maybe there are other reasons. I'll write more on this later when I've heard from you.

Sincerely,
Dr. Blake

April 5

Dear Jody,

I really believe the Christian message has an answer for each of the kids taking drugs whom I talked about in my last letter to you. Certainly when one becomes a believer in Christ he is immediately "in" and a part of a living body of Christ. (Remember the example of the hands and feet and eyes and taste buds when I wrote about the church being a body?) But more than this, he is also a new creation with a new outlook and new goals and a God-given love for others. The second group of drug users I mentioned were those who seek an escape; here again Christ provides the answer for the despair which pervades our culture. The weakest person is taken into the greatest power in the universe — through the Word of God, prayer, and the fellowship and encouragement of fellow believers, the world of despair is transformed into opportunities to love and serve others.

When we come to those who are looking for reality or God on an LSD trip, we meet head-on the innate desire of every man to know his Creator. St. Augustine said it so well long ago: "Thou has made us for thyself, and our heart is not quiet until it rests in thee." When the disciples came to our Lord and asked him to show them the Father, he said very simply, "I am the way, the truth, and the life; no man comes unto the Father, but by me."

I don't think your position should be either to condemn or condone those on campus who are taking drugs, but if you can recognize the basic needs that your friends are trying to satisfy, you have a wonderful opportunity to present Christ.

Why don't you try to come home for a weekend and let us get caught up?

Yours,
Dr. Blake

Dear Jody,

So your friends want to refine the argument about premarital sex. "What exactly is marriage? Is the piece of paper so essential, or is it sufficient for two people in love to honestly intend to have no other partner?" "If a couple by getting engaged has announced to the world that they intend to get married, why isn't it all right for them to have intercourse before the wedding ceremony?" I'll admit all of this sounds plausible on the surface, but love and marriage are more than surface phenomena. Just look at how many couples we both know here in town who announced their engagements with a splash of excitement, and then several months later quietly returned the gifts. Now most of them are married to someone else. I'm afraid that if permissive sex were the approved thing for engaged couples you would find many couples getting engaged, perhaps unconsciously, just for sex. It's just one stage beyond the approval of sex with "going steady" as I wrote about earlier.

The Christian view from earliest time has been complete abstinence from sex by both men and women before the marriage and complete faithfulness after the ceremony. The idea of a double standard for men and women is not found in the Bible. The Apostle Paul says it this way in Ephesians: "For this cause shall a man leave his father and his mother and shall cleave to his wife and they two shall be one flesh." I understand that "one flesh" really carries with it the meaning of one organism and that goes away beyond the sexual act. Two lives are intertwined in an inseparable union. They are bound up together in the bundle of life. It is more than being in love, more than sex, more than living happily ever after, although each of these is involved.

Let me know what you think.

Yours,
Dr. Blake

Dear Jody,

What I probably failed to get across in my last letter was that the Christian view of sex with its complete abstinence before marriage is more than a negative precept. It has very practical, down-to-earth positive value. The whole point is that marriage is composed of a great many things besides physical sex. There are lots of heartaches, sorrows, and troubles; there are bills to pay, wrinkled fenders, hospitals and doctors; there are sick babies, clothes to buy, a house to furnish. Of course, there are also times of happiness and success; there are mutual friends, coffee with neighbors, the PTA, church and Sunday school, vacations and play. All of the experiences of life together serve to strengthen the bonds of love so that the giving of each one to the other in sexual intercourse is the extension or the climax of all the other experiences of the union. You can't separate out sex and treat it alone and say, "Let's just enjoy this before the wedding," because it's related to the rest of the marriage experience which can't even be known until there is the mutual trust and confidence of marriage.

Imagine a football player going to the coach and saying, "I really enjoy the thrill of scoring touchdowns but I don't want to train or to go out for practice; just put me in to score the touchdowns." You know what the coach would say! The cheers of the stands and the applause of the press are given to the man who crosses the goal line, but every football player and every coach knows that discipline and training with all of the sweat and agony of practice are what result in touchdowns. For a man to say he wants no part of the team except for the moment of thrill of scoring would show that he doesn't understand team work or the purpose of the game. He wants to wrench the glory and the thrill out of context. The monstrosity of sex outside of marriage is that it is an attempt to wrench one part of the union from all the rest of the experiences which make up the one organism. Those who advocate or practice premarital or extramarital sex show they do not understand the purpose of the game.

Perhaps this will give you some answers for

your friends who raised the question in the first place. You can probably think of some better arguments, but at least you might start with the football player!

Dr. Blake

Dear Jody,

Just a note. I think the point you raise about the increase in venereal disease is an entirely different question; it relates to promiscuity and not to two sincere young people who have never had sexual relations before but find themselves engaged and ask, "Is this the time?" V.D. appears to be increasing, especially among the young, and in some areas of our culture it is reaching alarming rates. As you may remember, Mrs. Blake is a volunteer nurse in a clinic in a rescue mission which borders on Greenwich Village. Once a week the young people are invited in for a free meal and a worship service, and a medical clinic is available to them; venereal disease is rampant and it is common to find girls of fifteen or sixteen already infected. These young people have been caught up in the movement which rejects the establishment with all of its fences and safeguards, including morality. It is interesting to note that they turn to that same establishment when troubles come. But I think this is a subject we may want to talk about some other time, maybe when you come home for vacation. Perhaps you would even like to visit the clinic and see some of those who come in — poor, scared young people with real problems.

Cordially,
Dr. Blake

May 2

Dear Jody,

Your letter about the rock festival was one of the most interesting things I've read for some time. Why don't you consider writing it up for publication in one of the Christian magazines? Do you think anyone would believe it? It was interesting to me that a lot of the kids you talked to felt the glamor has worn off the Woodstock image.

I'm not sure Woodstock was as wonderful as many people would like to have us believe anyway. There's been a lot of talk about how much love there was and how the beautiful people got along so well caring for each other throughout the festival. The point people tend to overlook is that for three days this huge crowd of young people was completely divorced from the problems of the real world. The crowd was a narrow slice taken out of the middle of the best fed, best educated, most affluent society in history. They left behind all of the sick and the maimed, all of the mental hospitals, all of the old people who need attention and the babies who need to have their diapers changed, and for three days they got along fine.

The wonderful thing about the Christian gospel is that it reaches humanity in its entirety. It's not confined to a thin slice of healthy young, but it has meaning for the young and the old, the rich and the poor, the healthy and the sick. The promise of our Lord was not happiness for three days, but indescribable joy for eternity.

Dr. Blake

Dear Jody,

This is going to be short; I am writing it on my lunch hour. I didn't realize the professor you met at church, and that you have mentioned several times, is nearly fifty, and married. By all means, don't go out with him! I hear what you say about his being an active member in the church you are attending and I am sure he's a charming man of high reputation on campus. But Jody, please remember, underneath the impressive facade, he is still an ordinary fallen man.

Even if he weren't married, I would still be very cautious because of the difference in your ages — but to date a married man is absolutely out of the question. I know it doesn't help much to tell you this type of thing happens often but

you should know it's a well recognized phenomenon among marriage counselors. Perhaps you
should talk to the pastor of your church; he may
be able to help. In the meantime, don't let yourself be used as a pawn in this man's flight from
reality.

I'm really concerned,
Dr. Blake

Dear Jody,

I can't tell you how glad I was to have your letter telling me you are going out with David again. He may not be as sophisticated as your professor friend, but give him twenty to thirty years and he probably will run rings around him.

I am not jumping to the conclusion that you're going to marry David just because you are going out with him, but there are some things I'd like to say to follow up my recent letters about marriage. One of the wonderful things about two lives together is the way a couple learns together and grows together. I think it's particularly important that the wife grow with her husband. I've seen too many intelligent, vivacious young brides get bogged down in housework and the babies and sadly watch their husbands grow away from them. Resolve now not to let that happen to you. I'm glad David is a Christian and, of course, this makes the possibility for growth together all the more wonderful.

By all means, you have my permission to let David read my letter about the football player who only wanted to score touchdowns. I'm sort of pleased that you still have it.

Sincerely yours,
Dr. Blake

Dear Jody,

I really don't know how to reply to your last letter. Mrs. Blake and I have been looking forward to having your help with the young people during summer vacation and now it looks as if you will be in South America. I just can't understand how it happened so quickly, but I'm glad you prayed about it and that you have peace in your decision.

As you know, I strongly recommend a period of short-term missionary work for young people and while yours will not be for the two years I usually suggest, it will still have many of the benefits. How better can you learn what a missionary's life is all about? You can't be expected to solve a lot of problems, but you certainly will be able to see firsthand what some of them are.

Your decision to work in a hospital rather than a rural school is, I think, very wise. This way you will get some good experience to help in your decision of whether or not you should go to nursing school and I am sure that your love and kindness will shine through even though you think your Spanish isn't as good as it should be. Are you going to be home even for a day? If not, be sure to send us your address so we can write to you. I won't expect a lot of letters with such a full schedule, but be sure to take pictures and we'll have a get-together of our old class when you come back in the fall. May God bless you and use you. I know he will.

Mrs. Blake joins me in wishing you a very successful summer in every way.

Sincere best wishes,
Dr. Blake